All Scripture references taken from the KJV of the Holy Bible, unless otherwise indicated.

Seducing Spirits *Idolatry & Whoredoms*

by Dr. Marlene Miles

Freshwater Press 2024

freshwaterpress9@gmail.com

ISBN: 978-1-963164-80-0

Paperback Version

Table of Contents

Seducing Spirits:
Idolatry & Whoredoms

Freshwater Press, USA

In the latter times,
some shall depart from the faith,
giving heed to *seducing* spirits.
(1 Timothy 4:1)

Introduction

I am writing these things to you about those
who are trying to lead you astray.
(1 John 2:26)

If you are resistant to doing a certain
thing--, say a crime or sin, you may have to
be *seduced* in order to commit that
transgression. We see movie after movie
where some mastermind gives the talk to a
crew of people to convince them to go in
with him to commit a heist. They want to
score the money, the gold, or the diamonds,
usually.

That's in the natural, but when sins-
-, when spiritual infractions are committed
the <u>human being</u> is the heist. Either
something they own, are *about* to be blessed
with, a skill, virtue, gift, ability, marriage,

child, or some future benevolence from God is the heist.

The sad thing is that without even being aware of it, one can be *seduced;* he or she may be coerced or tricked into doing something that opens them up for the grand theft. Worse than that, many times humans don't even know they've been ripped off until much later. Sometimes they don't know it until it is too late.

If, like Jesus we could **feel virtue leave us**, we'd know right away that we've been drained of something. We would repent quickly and pray earnestly for restoration of whatever we've lost or whatever has been stolen from us. Instead, we humans may only feel what we *think* we **gained** from sins we have committed alone, or interactions that we have had with others while we bask in our flesh.

Instead, if we were in the spirit, first we wouldn't have sinned, moreover we would be convicted and or apprised by the Holy Spirit that we did just sin, and also that we just LOST something in the transaction.

Even being invited and enticed to sin where we really don't want to or plan to sin we must be seduced. That seduction is to get us to give up chastity, virtue, or steal some other thing from us. To be seduced there must be something in us that connects with the words and or actions of the *seducer*. This book is about the *seducing spirit*, but it is also about it's partner *spirit* or *spirits* that cause mankind to hear, receive, respond to, and connect with that *seducing spirit.*

Ask yourself, what *spirit* in me is bearing witness with a *seducing spirit?* Listen, hear God and then get rid of it!

Jesus was taken up on a high place and tempted of the devil at one point in the Gospels. He passed every one of those temptations. At another point in the Gospels Jesus said, **Hereafter I will not talk much with you: for the prince of this world cometh, and hath nothing in me**, (John 14:30).

My point? Seducing words can fly all around you, but if there is nothing in you

8

that identifies with or connects with words of seduction, it just won't touch you. It just won't. When we think of seduction we think of sex, and what connects with free and liberal sex is *whoredom* or *whoredoms*, fornication, adultery, prostitution, harlotry in the natural. In the spirit when these acts are committed God refers to idolatry as *whoredom* and *whoredoms*. In this book you will see *seducing spirit* and *whoredom* or *whoredoms* used interchangeably to describe adultery and spiritual adultery against God, which we know is idolatry.

At the end we have prayers against all of this so we all can be delivered and set free, so we can, like Jesus, declare that *the prince of this world has nothing in me*. With this as the case, we will be able to hear seducing words, and clearly be able to hear them for what they are and never be deceived. In our day-to-day life, we may see seducing images and either turn our head and not lock into those images and be captured by them. We may see people performing seductive acts and not be attracted to them, but instead repulsed by them. We will flee youthful lusts. We will resist the devil and he will flee from us.

In this way we will be victorious, not fall for demonic temptations and we will bring Glory to God.

Amen.

Whoredoms

The spirit of whoredoms is a strongman that can reign over an individual, over a family as in collective captivity. It can even rule over churches. Over churches? That may make one think that that particular church is some kind of filthy sex den. Well, *whoredoms* is what you think it is, but it is about so much more than sex, as we will learn. Because of this a church can be encumbered by *whoredoms* but not involved in sex sins in anyway.

In Hosea 4:12 we see that this *spirit* caused God's people to err, to go astray, to be deceived, to be seduced, to be made to stagger and cause to wander. Families, groups and even churches can be under this bondage collectively.

Strong's Concordance defines the *spirit of whoredoms* as committing spiritual adultery or fornication on a continual and wholesale basis. To play the harlot or in the case of the one who is chasing harlots or chasing normal chaste people to turn them into harlots by defilement. Spiritual oppressions and possessions are like blatant or hidden diseases that want to spread like viruses and filthy bacteria.

Whoredoms in a person makes them go-a-*whoring*. In the world, this is celebrated by immature and unsaved males, especially. Men are encouraged to sow their wild oats. Folks, if a man has even one wild oat, not to mention many, he should submit for deliverance instead of spreading them. In so doing he is d'evangelizing for the devil. The person with the wild oats should ask himself, why are his *oats* **wild**? What is something **wild** or of unknown origin_doing in a man of God?

At night the enemy sows weeds so anything wild should be removed, not passed on to another unsuspecting soul.

The devil's goal is to defile the one who is **not** a harlot; virgins come to mind. If this were a video game, I'm sure more points would be given for contaminating a virgin or otherwise good girl than one who is already sexually promiscuous. Gender-wise, vice versa; women can be on assignment to spoil good guys and good men as well.

Then the cover becomes that the man with the *wild oats* is dating a good girl, then he must be a good guy, because everyone knows that if you are seen with a harlot then you must be a harlot chaser or a whoremonger. Even whoremongers don't want that reputation in public, but will brag about their *body count* in private with their bruhs or whatever devil will listen to them.

We all have sinned and fallen short of the glory of God; we all have made mistakes. Some of us have made more than one mistake and many may have made the same mistake more than once; I know I have. Thank God for His forgiveness, but having or being under the *spirit of whoredoms* means that you continually and without repentance do these sorts of things.

If you are speeding in your vehicle, just once or for a little distance, you most likely won't get a ticket, but if you maintain a speeding velocity for at least ¼ mile or some other predetermined distance, you may be pulled over and ticketed. There is some grace, even in the world.

Making a mistake and repenting for it is one thing, but whoring after idols on a continual basis is *whoredoms*.

My people ask counsel at their stocks, and their staff declareth unto them: for the spirit of whoredoms hath caused them to err, and they have gone a whoring from under their God." (Hosea 4:12)

We all know what *whoredoms* is in the physical sense, and we think mostly of it in a sexual way. In the physical, *whoredoms* is when someone is lusty and hot in the pants. Flesh acts are common.

A narcissist has no concept that he is causing pain to others by pleasing their own lust; they only care about themselves. They often objectify others believing they are the only ones who are human and have feelings. Everyone else is just objects like game pieces to be moved about on a game board as in checkers or if you're really intelligent, and most narcissists believe they are--, a chessboard.

One who is caught up in *whoredoms* is someone who has not been faithful to abstain from fulfilling the lust of the flesh. It is someone who cares not that their selfish actions break the heart of God, their **First Love**, which is Christ who gave all for us, His bride.

For I am jealous over you with godly jealousy: for I have espoused you to one (spiritual) husband, that I may present you as a chaste virgin to Christ.
(2 Corinthians 11:2)

The *spirit of whoredoms* is in operation when saved folks indulge the lust of the flesh, even if only once. As evidenced in multiple books of the Bible, and

15

especially Hosea. This breaks God's heart. Even saved folks can sin, as you must know. Sins are by temptation and invitation--, *sinvitation* is what I call it. Sin is also with the escort of the demon that invited you. Blame it on another human all you want, there was at least one demon involved.

Temptations may seem small, or they may be huge. Lasagna arrives at the office for free because today you have declared a personal fast or you are part of a corporate fast. The best-looking guy you've ever seen in your life wants to have sex with you, and he's been wooing you for months, so you believe him. Those are both temptations to *whoredoms*, and they are both serious.

Sadly, sin often feels good while you are in the process of it, while you are in the throes of passion, for example.

If you say *It's my body, it's my life* while doing some or every flesh thing you feel like doing, declaring yourself the captain of your own vessel, ignoring the Word and the Will of God, you are working *whoredoms*.

Idolatry first begins with oneself. It begins with *I want, I need, or I must have. I am most important. I need it now. I can't do without that.*

Idolatry, of which *whoredoms* is a part, is a person pleasing themselves over God and over everyone else. Idolatry is the worship of anything, especially something made by man's hand as a *god*. Idolatry is not giving worship that should go to God to God but instead to something or someone else. Idolatry is part of *whoredoms*. If the *spirit of whoredoms* is not in you or in your ancestry, foundation, or bloodline, you would not worship any idol. Not one.

Scorched Earth people do what they like. Tyrants do what they like and make others do what the tyrant wants done. Pharaohs were the same; they were tyrants. When one person is having their way at the expense of another, others, or the many, without regard to the Will of God, they are moving in *whoredoms* and showing how much they love themselves and themselves alone. They are narcissists.

I know thy works, and thy labour, ..., and how thou canst not bear them which are evil: and thou hast tried them which say they are apostles, and are not, and hast found them liars: ...
and for my name's sake hast laboured, and hast not fainted. Nevertheless I have somewhat against thee, because thou hast left thy first love.
Remember ... from whence thou art fallen, and repent, and do the first works; or else I will come unto thee quickly, and will remove thy candlestick out of his place, except thou repent.
(Revelation 2:2-5 *emphasis, mine*)

This is what a letter from God would look like when a person has lost his *first love*. This is what was written to the Church at Ephesus in the Book of Revelation. Even though all other kinds of good works and deeds are being done by that person, or in that Church, in this case for the Kingdom, if he, she, or She has moved into idolatry, they've lost their **First Love**. A person (or church) could be prayerful--, praying up a storm, it could be generous, feeding the poor, and visiting those in prisons and also visiting the sick and shut-in, but if this church has a secret sin and that sin is idolatry, their final report will show that the secret sin negated all the other good things about that person (or church). Idolatry is the same as having an illegal lover in the natural. That hurts your spouse so much.

We give worship to idols when we do what *they* want us to do. We don't have to guess what that is--, anything an idol suggests will be in direct opposition to what the Lord says, what the Bible says, and it will be opposite of what pleases the heart of God. Just as an illegal lover will not suggest you be good to, pay attention to, or *stay* with your legal spouse, but instead will try to draw you to themselves.

If you see a man or woman steeped in idolatry that person is a top candidate for *whoredoms* because idolatry is a part of *whoredoms*. If you see a man involved in any type of *whoredoms*, be assured they have idols somewhere. Spouses and spouses-to-be, your mate is less likely to cheat if they are not steeped in idolatry or have lots of idols. If you are the one saturated in idolatry, get delivered from idolatry, as well as from *whoredoms*.

Stick with your *first love*; learn how to love one and love that one very well and with your whole being, as God instructs. If you can love God properly and put Him in His proper place in your life, then being successfully married to another who can also do that will be a cinch.

When you are hurting humans by idolatry, that is, cheating on them, there may be hell to pay from your spouse. When we cheat on God, the difference is that God operates in Mercy and Grace, whereas humans may not. Idols have no Mercy; the same idol that led you into sin will retaliate against you if you don't do what they require or demand; and they do this by influencing other humans to act out against you, for them, as they have no bodies. The idol wants you to sin by continuing idol worship, and will punish you if you do not.

What have you gotten yourself into?

The Seducing Spirit

Ooh, ooh, ooh, I will go and be a lying spirit and trick him. Lying spirits are *seducing spirits*; liars are seducers.

The serpent seduced Eve with words, imagery, lies, and I believe repeated visitations like a constant drip until she gave in. Seriously folks, how many times will a male visit a female to try to get her **to eat an *apple*?** When the devil visits it's to entice a person into some kind of sin; and why not idolatry, since God hates it the most?

Parents: would you kick your child out of the house for eating an *apple*? Would you kick your child out of the house for eating any food, even the last of the ice cream or their little brother's birthday cake?

And if you did, would you post an angel with a flaming sword that turned every which way to keep them out of the *house*?

For thought: *Perhaps eating of the Tree of the Knowledge of Good and evil could be described as idol-a-tree?* Could that be why the punishment to Adam and Eve was so swift and so harsh?

Delilah seduced Samson with sex. Samson liked women, so the devil already knew what to use to tempt him.

Did Tamar seduce Judah on his way to Timnah (Gen 38:14), or had the devil already seduced Judah and Judah was just looking for *opportunity*? Not to be funny, but the men who got with Tamar died so we don't know if that would have scared Judah away or piqued his curiosity about her. We do know he wasn't sending in his last son to try to raise up an heir to the firstborn son Er. That's why Tamar, possibly under the influence of a *seducing spirit,* believed she was taking matters into her own hands, changed into a seductive outfit and set out to Enaim to sleep with Judah. After all, she may have thought, Judah had three boys, so he made *boys*—and she needed a boy. And, obviously Judah wasn't the type to *pull out*.

The devil tried to seduce Jesus with power, fame, accomplishments, and food. All of those things fall under *whoredoms*. Seduction doesn't always involve sex. A person can be seduced or induced to do something that they may not ordinarily do for money, power, fame, or status.

The devil fulfills the evil requests of those who want **spiritual power.** Power belongs to God so the devil can't give Godly power to anyone, but he sure has a counterfeit; he gives demonic power to those who will serve him in exchange for --, well, pretty much everything.

Jezebel seduced the prophets who ate at her table. Food can be seductive; some foods are considered aphrodisiacs. Food can be bewitched. There is food that has been sacrificed to idols, food dedicated to ancestors—especially the meat. Don't eat unknown food—either what it is, or where it came from. Don't eat spiritual food of any kind, in the dream. None of the above should be eaten. Regular, ordinary food should not be eaten until it is blessed, prayed over, even sanctified with thanksgiving to God.

People can become connected to ancestral altars by the eating of meat sacrificed to the dead. Another translation says the food sacrificed to idols.

They yoked themselves to the Baal of Peor and ate sacrifices offered to lifeless gods;
(Psalm 106:28)

To seduce, means to draw aside from the path of righteousness and duty, by flattery, promises, bribes or otherwise; to tempt and lead to iniquity; to corrupt; to deprave. The physical attributes of a woman and what she wears to enhance her appearance of the same is seduction.

To seduce also means to entice to a surrender of chastity which is to make a person have sex with you.

A college fellow called his own apartment a *seductorium*--, a made-up word, for sure, but that was what he planned to do in his apartment every chance he got—seduce women.

A **seducer** seduces by temptation, the black arts, by promises, and even lies. The seducer can be male or female. This *seducer* is a little less criminal than a murderer because when people have sex, they open up their soul to the other person. How that person respects or disrespects the other person's soul determines how and if that soul will thrive, survive or even be murdered. A soul can be murdered. A person you are not married to should never be entrusted with your **soul** or your body.

A seducer is also a person or thing which leads astray. He, she, or it entices another or others to evil, causing them to fall into error. *Error* seduces one into **more error** which may lead to destruction.

Folks Learn Seduction

"Come and go with me. It'll be fun. It won't hurt. No one will find out. It's not hurting anyone." Beware of the words of a seducer. It is not always that simple or that out in the open. There are people who covertly seduce and groom the unsuspecting or law-abiding, and the God-abiding types into crimes and sins.

There are manipulators and there are master manipulators. Either is scary. Powers of seduction and charm are learned, earned, and can be purchased, from the devil or one of his agents at one of his numerous *franchises*, by the selling of one's own soul. A person may not realize that they've sold their soul, they may only know that they want what they want so badly that they are willing to do anything to get that something that they want. The phrase that indicates desperation is heard when a person says *they'll do anything for---*. Those words should never come out of anyone's mouth. **Never**.

The *seducing spirit* is a very powerful one that appeals to the flesh or soul of the intended victim. That *seducing spirit* has reconnoitered the intended victim and knows what they lack and what they like. They know what that person wants to hear and needs to hear to be pliable in the hands of the perpetrator. The charm and the seduction are demonically charged. There is a devil anointing that the innocent may not be able to discern, hear, sense, see, or resist. Truthfully, the victim may not *want* to see through this. After all, finally someone is making their dreams come true saying and doing all the romantic things that they've imagined, possibly for years.

It's a play. Act One or Act Done, it doesn't matter, the would-be perp is playing his part beautifully. And she may not even want to take the intermission between the acts; she may want it to keep going.

(Oh fairytales, look what you've done to us!)

Whoredoms doesn't have to be about sex; a person can be seduced into parting with their money as in sympathy ploys so the person gives to magnanimous causes or be seduced by the desire to be rich or famous and so give money to the person who is promising that.

Any part or many parts of a person can be charmed by the devil to make that perpetrator irresistible, or nearly so. That human victim or would-be victim has been studied and monitored, and the *monitoring* or *familiar spirit* has reported back to the person who is giving the seducer the charm anointing, or creating a physical *charm* to work against his intended victim. In this way, the seducer is actually a **weapon** against another person--, her body, her life, her destiny. But she is enjoying it--, at least, at first.

(Still, we say, No weapon formed... a **person** can be a weapon, saints of God!)

A seducer may use a charm. A charm is not the same as a cute ornament that hangs from a bracelet or a gold neck chain, it is a demonic device created usually by a witch or witch doctor. It can be anything from a liquid love potion to a physical device that when placed and or activated the intended victim will do just what the charm intends that they do. It is either for manipulation, affliction, or even death.

Folks, you have to stay prayed up.

With or without a physical *charm*, a seducer with a *seducing spirit* will have a person thinking that they are the **only person in the entire world**, and if the victim needs to believe that, or wants to believe that, then they will. Ofttimes, the perp love bombs and makes romantic moves as quickly as possible especially if they are hiding some heinous, deal breaking flaw, or agenda that they don't want the intended to find out about. For example, the perp may love bomb in order to earn a person's trust so they can steal money from them.

When some time or events have gone by the victim may wonder, *What was I thinking?* It may not be until then that the person realizes that they were indeed under a spell--, under the spell of the seducer. And, they may have been led away into error in their thinking and actions, believing and doing things that they would not ordinarily do while they were under the control of a seducer.

How much *charm* is in a demonic charm? How much power does a *seducing spirit* have? It depends on their relationship with the dark kingdom, that is, what level of witch they are, or what level of witch they have visited to get this seducing power. What devil deal have they made if they are their own evil human agent?

It is also dependent on how important is the taking down, derailing, interfering with, stealing from, killing, or destroying the intended victim or his destiny. The devil will give at least the amount of power needed based on the perp's intentions. Oh, folks, none of this stuff is free. The amount of power in the charm is dependent on the value of the sacrifice put on the demonic altar. That value is subjective since the demon decides what or how much the person should bring. No matter what he brings, that's only a down payment because this is never paid in full, more will be required of the person wanting the charm or potion--, so much more, into the generations of that person. Demons want life and they want blood.

How easy or difficult will it be? That will also speak to how much demonic power will be in a *charm*. No matter what power is in it, if the intended victim has no spiritual walls up and this charm is spiritually unopposed, the person may be devastated by it.

If we are looking at an unsaved person, or a dry Christian, that will be easier than if the target is a prayed up, sanctified, set-aside child of God who is hot in prayers day and night and also in the noon day. A person who reads and studies the Word, fasts, praises, worships and seeks God will be very difficult to unseat or disrupt, so the enemy may give a strong or stronger level of deceptive ability to the perpetrator who is trying to overcome a **real** Christian.

For there shall arise false Christs, and false prophets, and shall shew great signs and wonders; insomuch that, if it were possible, they shall deceive the very elect.
(Matthew 24:24)

Most of us want to be liked and valued. So, when someone shows us attention or behaves toward us in a way that invites us to feel somewhat special, we're likely to be drawn to them to a degree. And we almost never assume the person is mounting a calculated "charm offensive" merely to get something they want or that perhaps they even have intent to take advantage of us in some way. Rather, we'd like to think there's something really remarkable about us that is motivating the person to love us or be head over heels over us because---, finally *my love has come along.*

Go ahead and live a while, you may be able to spot an old charmer a mile off. An old G? No problem, you will be able to see through their *game* as well—that is if you have experience, but a young, innocent or naïve person may not be able to discern lie from truth. It is difficult without discernment *via* the Holy Spirit to tell the difference between benign charm and evil seduction. This is one of the many reasons why young innocents are targeted; they may not have the wherewithal to spot a lie as easily as a seasoned person may.

As before said, some can know that they are being seduced and they like it. We shouldn't like it, but our flesh does. Our ego does. Our lust does. Our greed does. Our pride likes it because we can brag to friends about are appeal to the opposite gender.

Those under the influence of *seducing spirits* will come to steal kill and destroy, and they do this by any means necessary. They will lie, cheat, and manipulate to get what they want from the person – whatever that is. Sometimes it's whatever they can get, just to have the feeling that they *scored*. Sometimes it is something in particular. Sometimes they want everything from you. *Everything*.

What are you willing to lose or risk losing just to have your ego stroked by a *seducer* who is under the influence of a *seducing spirit*?

The answer should be nothing.

Is it?

Do not trust a flattering tongue.
For neither at any time used we flattering words, as ye know, nor a cloke of covetousness; God is witness: (1 Thessalonians 2:5)

When an evil seduction is so successful that one is swept off of one's feet—careful, they say that the serpent in the Garden used to have feet, therefore, to become footless is a curse. To have no footing is to be tossed about by winds of doctrine. To have no footing is to have no foundation, and nothing can be built without a proper foundation. So, don't sin to let yourself fall under curses. Keep your feet; do not let anyone sweep yours from under you.

In the hair salon today, the discussion was about the wonderful things men have said to women. All but one woman said that no man has ever made her any such promises, but most of the women there say that the men they've met have all said things like, *No, you don't have to work, I'll take care of you. I got you; I'll pay all your bills.* So many men do not want their wives to work--, until they do. I'd venture that 90% of women who are told that they can be stay-at-home wives and the man will take care of everything will marry that man even with all his warts, and not even notice that he has warts. Those are seducing words to the woman who wants to stay home and manage the house and take care of the children that they plan to have.

In the natural, inconsistent behavior in a person should be noted. The person who can't maintain whatever character they are presenting themselves to be is most likely acting. Pay attention to red flags and whatever visceral feeling you get when something is not right. In this way you might spot a seducer operating under a *seducing spirit.*

I get nausea in my belly when something is spiritually wrong, and I hate nausea. That is my *discerner* speaking to me in the language that I will heed and do something about. My discerner can be your discerner too; He is the Holy Spirit of God.

Some *Want* to Be Seduced

Itching ears, want to hear something new, sometimes they want to hear something outrageous. Adventure seekers want to be wowed, and if they take this too far, or if this is in their blood, they may seek out *seducers* without realizing it.

Nevertheless, I have this against you: You tolerate that woman Jezebel, who calls herself a prophet. By her teaching she misleads my servants into sexual immorality and the eating of food sacrificed to idols. (Revelations 2:20)

The above verse was written to the Church at Thyatira and clearly says that woman, Jezebel. Jezebel is a spirit; it is neither male nor female. A man can have the *spirit of Jezebel*; it is the *spirit of witchcrafts.* Women as teachers are not disallowed in the Kingdom of God, else God wouldn't have called any female teachers. I walk in a serious teacher's anointing; when I teach I am alive. That gift is from God. Just know that if Jezebel is present there is an Ahab as well; either spirit can be in either gender. Don't be mysogynistic; because God isn't. *Thank you.*

Many people think that if they are seduced or induced to do a thing—even a sin or something that they would not normally do that they will go Scot free, blaming the one who made them do it. Folks who secretly want to sin want to be seduced, planning to use the fact that they were enticed or encouraged by another to do this crime or sin as a defense. When a person wants to sin, it is built in that they are figuring out how to get away with it, often *before* the transgression.

Back in the day, comedian Flip Wilson created a character, Geraldine, who constantly said, *The devil made me do it.* The devil is always behind sins that people do. For this reason people who want to do bad things but get away with it want to be seduced, thinking that's a loophole.

It's not. Being seduced in no way limits complicity. All sins are by invitation and demonic escort; surely God's eyes are on the demon, but the demon is doing what the demon is supposed to be doing—*demon stuff,* such as *stealing, killing, and destroying.* **You**, on the other hand, are a child of God and you are not supposed to be acting like any demon that has come into your life and your very soul to impart it's nature to you. It's nature is sin; it is where sin nature comes from.

When folks are doing exactly what they want to do, it looks something like this:

They will not frame their doings to turn unto their God: for the spirit of whoredoms is in the midst of them, and they have not known the Lord.
(Hosea 5:4)

If you buy something *hot (stolen)* from a thief or middleman, **you** are not innocent. That low price on the Rolex seduced you, and you were induced to pay

39

the thief so much money for the opportunity to wear that status timepiece. You are not innocent. Now, if he didn't steal the Rolex and it is really a Rolox; it's a knock off and you gave him 2K for a $19 fake, you're the one who was again duped into **error**. It's still seduction on the part of the salesperson and it is still *whoredoms* in you taking the bait.

Sin is hot. It's hot in a hellish way.

But sin is also hot in that the power to seduce or induce a person to sin came from God. Fallen angels did not create themselves nor did they empower themselves. Power belongs to God; all power all came <u>from</u> God. The only thing fallen angels (devils, demons, and idol *gods*) did was to fall from Heaven with full intent to uses the stolen power that they stole from God against God by using it against God's people.

Saints of God, if *whoredoms* is in you it is ATTRACTING *seducing spirits* because you are marked for it, you are susceptible to it. You need to do a lot of foundation work, or you will keep attracting the same stuff over and over.

In this way you are being stolen from, lied to, enticed by lust to look rich or well off and made a fool of and worst of all WORSHIPPING *whoredoms*, making it grow larger in you, enlarging your flesh man as well. Stolen or not, hot or not, shopping excursions and feasts for the eye, belly, soul, fame, power, and sexual organs grow *whoredoms* in your soul by giving worship to that demon *spirit*. This is how the *spirit* can grow into a strongman, block the gates of your family line, and span generations in your bloodline.

Don't be the one to invite it into your family. Don't be the one to feed it if you realize that it is afflicting or oppressing you. Don't be the one to keep it around. Resist the devil and he will flee from you. Don't feed the *seducing spirit of whoredoms*.

Ezekiel 16

*The following 24 sections with
numbered Verses are not the
chronological verses of Ezekiel 16,
but they are selected verses from the
Book of Ezekiel that describe
whoredoms with both a natural and
spiritual application.*

Verse 4

Rejection from the womb is a result of *whoredoms*. The world calls a baby born out of wedlock a *love child*, but a child of *whoredoms* is often not wanted and there may not have been any love involved, whatsoever.

They say a child can feel that rejection even in the womb. Some say it will bring on asthma in a child, especially if the parents have been constantly arguing. The *love child* is denied; the father may get up from that romp in the hay and declare, *It's not mine*.

The woman, feeling desperate or let down may try unsuccessfully to get rid of the pregnancy. If she lives, the child may also, but still be a source of pain and torment to either or both parents. The *love child* is expensive to whomever has to pay the fees for pregnancy, gestation, birth, upbringing, and upkeep.

The child is rejected, and the child knows it. The *love child* is the result of illegal, unsanctioned, unsanctified sex and that is because of *whoredoms*. The child is conceived in sin and shaped in iniquity, even with married, loving parents, but all the more with parents who came together because of seduction and *whoredoms*. It is not the child's doing or fault, it is purely on one or both of those people of child-bearing age.

The *love child* receives the curse of the bastard. Where is his father? If he is fatherless then he is considered a bastard. If he is unclaimed by his father, he is considered a bastard and inherits a curse. The following is Bible:

A bastard shall not enter into the congregation of the Lord; even to his tenth generation shall he not enter into the

congregation of the Lord.
(Deuteronomy 23:2)
But if ye be without chastisement,
whereof all are partakers, then are
ye bastards, and not sons.
(Hebrews 12:8)

The saving Grace is that in Christ, when your natural father or mother forsake you, the Lord will take you up. So even if we were born fatherless, we don't have to remain so. If we were even rejected at birth, the Lord will still take us as His own. We can be adopted into the family of God and enjoy a Heavenly Father who will watch over, provide for and take care of us in every way.

When my father and my mother forsake
me, then the Lord will take me up.
(Psalm 27:10)

The following prayer points are from my book, **SON**.

- Father, in the Name of Jesus Christ, forgive me and my ancestors going back at least 10 generations for all fornications, rapes, incest, especially those by which children were conceived, and allowed the curse of the bastard to fall on us.

- I forgive those that raped or molested me or any of my ancestors, in the Name of Jesus.
- Lord, forgive these sins, wash me with the Blood of Jesus Christ, thereby removing all iniquity in my family line, in the Name of Jesus. Amen.

Verse 5

None eye pitied thee, to do any of these
unto thee, to have compassion upon thee;
but thou wast cast out in the open field, to
the lothing of thy person, in the day that
thou wast born.

We should not be judgmental but
many of us have seen kids that no one is
paying any attention to. Their so-called
parent may be present, but completely
ignoring their own child, leaving the child
to their own *devices*. Many times, those
devices are literally *devices*; the TV, the
game consoles, and cartoons streaming on
the cell phone. This child is being raised by
online content or no one at all. That is the
child that is *thrown out*, even if they live in
a house with parents. That is the child that

is love-starved, attention-starved, conversation-starved and often, touch-starved. It is a known fact that humans don't thrive if they are not touched (properly) from birth, if they are not talked to, if they do not interact with others in the right way at the right times in their lives.

As a reflex reaction that person begins to crave attention, time, touch. Ain't it just like the devil, though to create a problem, to create a deficit in a person's life and then offer to fill it by sending in what *looks like* the answer. Simply because they are not God, they either don't know what is needed--, God knows you, they don't really and don't really care to get to know you, expect to steal from you, hurt, kill or destroy you. So, the devil and his crew may cruelly send in the **opposite** of what is needed to "help" you solve the problem that the devil caused in your life in the first place. This seduction is entrapment.

The devil caused it you may ask?

Yes. Surely God didn't cause a child to be tossed out into a field and ignored. No, the devil sees a human when they are down and comes to drive the nail in the rest of the way. When God sees a person down, He has compassion on them and sends help from the Sanctuary or from the Throne of God to properly correct the problem and bring deliverance.

The evil *spirits* within a person, because of all the hurt and unmet needs may lead to sadness and sadness may lead to grief, feelings of depression or feelings of revenge, and any combination of all of that, or worse. *Whoredoms* gets a greater foothold on a person's life who is going through all that pain. *Whoredoms* convinces a person that if they get more boyfriends, girlfriends, stuff, things, money, fame, sex, or popularity they will feel better, be better, and be healed of all the emotional and spiritual pain they are feeling.

None of that is true. The pain will continue.

Eventually this pain manifests in the natural and the person may begin to experience physical pain in their body--, even chronic pain. Depression, for example, really **hurts**. Any normal person would want that pain to go away. Chronic or acute pain that doesn't seem to resolve may lead a person to despair and distress. Desperation opens the door for the devil. *Things and stuff,* or even revenge won't fix this, but a person with or without the Holy Spirit who is instead listening to demons will be deceived. Period.

Verse 15

Trusting in your own beauty or trusting in what the Lord has given you or done for you is a function of *whoredoms*. Someone once said to me, *"If you've got it, flaunt it."* That didn't register with my spirit. Her *whoredoms* was speaking and I didn't have *whoredoms* to answer hers.

Verse 15 is about playing the harlot and pouring out fornications on everyone who passes by. Some people have sex—any or every kind of sex because they *can--*, because of *whoredoms* and *lust*.

Spiritually, false teachings will be received and passed on. Discernment or the ability to judge right from wrong, knowing love from hate and truth from lie is gone out the window somewhere. Spirits will be transferred, and the wasting of God-given talents will be evident. Under this *seducing spirit*, the *spirit of whoredoms* it's as though anything goes.

The victim's discernment and their *"No"* may be gone, it may have been taken away years ago. They are like a city with no walls. They have set few to no boundaries and they can be talked into or out of almost anything.

Those who know have sometimes described their God given beauty as a curse. Narcissists don't describe it that way, but flaunt it. There is a balance in between as a man ought not to think more of himself than he ought.

A college girl couldn't get the attention of the boy she wanted and finally gave up saying, *"He acts a lot better looking than he is."* Without saying it she was saying he's a narcissist.

Sounds like sour grapes, but that man took whatever virtues or gifts he has and ran with that not looking back to what he lost or feels he doesn't have. He only focused on what he had and magnified it to the max. He was quite content and confident in his whoredoms--, so much so, it attracted the girl that wanted to date him.

If the emperor believes he has on new clothes, then in his mind he does. The mind is powerful. As that fellow continued to "act" good looking, soon he *was* good looking in the eyes of so many women--, even though he wasn't actually good looking. Eventually, he was respected by many (corrupt, unsaved) men for his *way* with the ladies.

Was Hugh Hefner attractive? How many men with money were perceived as attractive when they were not, really? How many celebrities are presented as attractive, and they are not? Some actors wore heavy makeup and were in soft focus before AI ever got a foothold, but those people exuded confidence, at least in public and on the stage and screen. How they were at home was another whole thing, but if they believed in themselves, then somehow they were able to convince the audience of the same. Don't be an audience, don't just be a spectator; be a discerner.

Verse 16

Do not love the world. If Jesus had loved the world and worldliness He would have lost in the Wilderness Temptations. What is so amazing to me is that Jesus came to Earth with **Love** for us, for mankind, and it was the Love that the Father gave Him for us. But at the same time, Jesus had no love for the world, that is, the *things and stuff* and trappings of this world.

We are charged in that same way, to love one another, but hate the world and worldliness. The dividing line, saints of God, is when the people we love are part of the world and cannot or will not separate themselves from it. Like the rich young ruler who would not sell all he had, give it to the poor and then follow Jesus. Like the rich man who was building more and more barns to hold all his harvests, but his soul was required of him that night. Obviously, God knew that man would never be separated from his wealth.

There is another danger here in that the rich man who has everything or believes he does, as soon as he comes into the Kingdom, he believes he comes in as a **ruler,** as if he's running things. He believes he comes in higher than those who are already in; that is not so in the Kingdom of God. Also, those who are already rich and rich in a worldly way may believe they can just *add* God or Church to their list of accomplishments. And, the already rich will let God know **that they made themselves** and not give God His glory. And, if that weren't enough, the worldly rich who are not willing to submit fully to God will bring the world or try to bring the world in with them because if they are rich and love money, then what are they willing to change, really? They won't change anything that got them money because that's their formula.

The Love God gives you is pure, it is righteous, it is *agape*; it is not worldly, of the world or for the world. We hate what God hates.

Unless Jesus had the right kind of Love, aimed at the right people, as soon as Jesus was baptized and filled with the Holy Spirit, He would have failed in the Wilderness.

But God so loved the world, you may argue. You are correct. He offered Love to all, and whosoever would forsake the world and follow Him, gave He the authority to become sons of God.

Spiritually, this evil *spirit* at work may be seen as decking the high places with colors and playing the harlot in the natural. When a person loves money, success, fame, and et cetera he may be giving money or gifts to false religious works or causes, to get what he wants, while woefully failing to maintain separation from the world. This is another trap and curse of *whoredoms*.

Verse 17

This *spirit* and/or strongman will lead a man to **worshipping men**, making idols or images of men and committing *whoredoms* with them. Idolizing men or teachers is one of the goals of this *seducing spirit*. Oh, foolish Galatians, who has bewitched you? It doesn't matter because if you are infected with the *spirit of whoredoms*, **almost anyone can bewitch you.** *Whoredoms* makes you look gullible, pliable, even desperate in the spirit.

A snake oil salesman can read you in the natural, walk up to you and tell you almost anything, and you will believe it. You may fall for all this stuff and so much more from Ezekiel 16, Hosea, and other books in the Bible.

We are born into the world and taught to idolize people, actors, actresses, supermodels, politicians, musicians, rich people. This is so not of God, yet it has invaded the church where pastors, singers, even whole choirs have and still endeavor to make a name for themselves. Jesus did not come to garner fame for Himself, yet others in the church do things with God-given gifts for fame and for money, which will in turn make them idols.

See that you, yourself do not seek the worship of men or become a worshipper of men.

Verse 18

Giving that which belongs to the Lord and what the Lord has given you to idols is *whoredoms*.

How so?

God gave you gifts, skills, and abilities. When you use those things for the **world**, that is *whoredoms*. When you use those things to please people, that is *whoredoms*, when you use those things to exalt yourself, that is still *whoredoms*. *Whoredoms* is what the devil wants you to use, or I shall say, waste your life on. If you don't give them up willingly, he has devised MANY ways to come and take, steal them from you or trick you into using what God gave you to the world, and for his benefit, not to bring glory to God. It is only when you are using gifts, skills, and abilities to bring Glory to God that you are doing why those virtues were given.

The issuing and success of a curse in any person's life is to induce them into sin and or destruction. The process may be quick or slow. *Whoredoms* is a number one tactic of the devil because sexual sin, especially, makes it super easy for the devil to introduce demons, devils, and idols into the soul of a person--, a man or a woman. There is no amount of smarts, savvy, or physical muscle power, or will power that can stop a spiritual attack as described. Even soulish desires of evil people get wrapped in spiritual devil anointing to make those desires power up and then fly in your direction to afflict and affect you. You will need spiritual weapons to fight demonic evil hurled at you.

Unfortunately, this stuff is invisible, and is only discerned by the Spirit of God. You need to hear and heed the Holy Spirit.

Verse 19

Sacrificing your sons and daughters to idols to be devoured by them may be a sad sequela of the *spirit of whoredoms.* Practicing false religions and joining cults especially because of intermarriage with the heathen is evident with this *spirit* as well. How many pagan women did Solomon marry, even after God told him not to?

I believe that a lot of sacrificing one's children to idols happens because of ignorance these days. Not always, because some evil parents know exactly what they are doing, but I believe a lot of it is ignorance. People really aren't spiritual and really are not wise as to what is evil initiation, evil dedication and what activities are truly demonic, even though they may be fun, and they want their children to experience certain things in their childhood because that's how they grew up. When this is happening, the idols are reproducing *after their kind* when you are performing family rituals and traditions because that's how you grew up, never learning another thing now that you are an adult and have children of your own.

Halloween is an evil initiation, yet we are seduced as children to get that candy. We may or may not care about the costumes, but the candy. Dressing your child as a demon, a witch, or any other character --, even a Bible character, on that particular day (or night), says in the spirit that you and your child are a part of what they are doing and then the season opens for demons, devils, and evil human agents to come after your child. Oh, that candy, that sugar rush introduces your child into *whoredoms* because who wouldn't want to feel good with a sugar high all the time?

Please don't do this.

Halloween is the highest "holy" day of witches and all things evil. Remember your mind can't fight this and neither can your child's little mind fight off the monsters in their room that they may actually be seeing that you are telling them is not real, so you can get some sleep because you are so tired. Your parents said the same to you because they were also tired. In so doing you turned off your spiritual senses and now you are teaching your child to do the same and be spiritually dull and ignorant.

I don't have to say, *Wake up!* I need to say, *WAKE BACK UP* to the way that God created you and designed you. Let the Holy Spirit wake your spirit man again and then begin to feed it with the Word of God!

Milk and cookies left for Santa is offering food to idols and that is idolatry. Recall, idolatry is part of *whoredoms*. If you are offering milk & cookies in exchange for gifts--, see how this goes? I could go on, but so much more is in my book, **This Is Not That:** ***How to Keep Demons from Coming At You.***

The devil is a legalist and if you offer your child to the devil, he will say, *Gotcha!* A carved pumpkin at the door of your house during Halloween tells the devil that he can have your youngest. And then he's got your child.

Surely, you didn't mean to do that, did you? Protect your child spiritually both in prayers and in knowledge, knowing right from wrong and using Wisdom to apply that knowledge.

Verse 24

Building brothels may literally mean the building of houses of ill-repute, but it can also mean building places where people will be made to feel good. This can include false ministries where people come in and get *krunk,* or whatever they get because now churches look like movie theaters—the stage is lit, the music is lit, the house lights are down.

If I am to go report to the priest so he can see me and I can get taught, healed, delivered, or whatever the Lord has for me there, then why are the house lights down? Oh, it's because the preacher and the musicians are putting on a show. That has got to be the reason.

Surely people who have something to hide are most comfortable in the dark, so why not turn out the lights in the place, so all the congregants can hide. Better make sure there are no pervs on the pews, it is now a dark theater, after all. God turns on the lights; the devil turns them off. If the preacher, the prophet or the priest doesn't want to **see** you, and you don't want to be seen either by God or His representatives then why are you there?

Whoredoms will have a person wanting the things of God and not wanting God. I want the feel-good moments of church, but if I come in some other way than the door, then I can hide in the dark.

Chasing *whoredoms* will make a person either build a high place to get what they want, circumventing God, or attempt to do so, or that person will frequent the high places. If that community is riddled with *whoredoms* there may be an evil altar on every street corner. Pay attention, in many cities that is the way it is.

Whoredoms also leads to idolatry of man, using God-given resources to build monuments to men. Monuments to men can also be built in the heart of a man where he has man-crushes, bromances, and idolatrous thoughts of one or many people. This man's (or woman's) idolatry can be secret or out in the open. Either way it is still idolatry and is the result of the *seducing spirit* of *whoredoms*. The devil has invited you to worship a person, a celebrity, a sports star, and you have answered something like, *Okay, I'll do it.*

Why?

You don't know; you've been seduced. Seduced is the same as bewitched. It felt good, you liked it, at least at first, or even still. It makes you feel important to be *identified* with someone famous, important, and or rich who doesn't even know you, wouldn't speak to you if they met you on the street and probably wouldn't throw their Diet Coke on you if you were on fire.

What the heck? It doesn't make sense and it doesn't have to make sense: you've been *seduced.*

The sad truth is the more people who worship a person the more star power that person has. The more likes, the more views, the more influence. It's because in that person's soul there is at least one demon who--- the more worship that demon gets, through the person that he's set up house in their soul, the happier the demon gets and the more power the demon garners from darkness and lends to the human idol that is being worshipped.

Star power, folks; that's how it works. Groupies are willing to physically chase and follow an idol, be that idol famous or a quiet individual, in that case it is called stalking, but the thrust of idolatry is still the same whether you physically follow a person or a group about, or just follow them online. If you are obsessed with everything they say and do, you are seduced and *whoredoms* is in you.

Verse 25

Be fruitful and multiply still stands in the Earth. I'm so enamored of that particular commandment and mandate of God that I wrote an entire book on it; **In Multiplying I Will Multiply Thee**. But the devil has found a way to multiply as well. He doesn't have souls, so he recruits. If you must be recruited and not born a certain way then you can know that the devil is in it.

The devil sponsors sin, promotes sin and multiplies *by* sin; it is how he recruits. In the natural we may think of the loose woman who makes herself available to all who come her way. Of course, this chapter is about Jerusalem playing the harlot and obviously cavorting with all that she encounters, but we are applying this chapter to *whoredoms* for individuals.

When a man is multiplying *whoredoms*, he may also be open to everyone who passes by, catches his eye or his fancy, but it is really the eye and the fancy of the demon or demons in his soul. Folks, it is not normal for a man or woman to go *a-whoring--*, God did not make us that way. That is a devil perversion.

A person who is open to everyone who passes by is also the person who eats at anyone's table. They may or may not be without discernment, but they are certainly without discretion. Spiritually, they may also be open to false pastors, false prophets, false teaching and teachers, and the doctrines of demons. He may be open to whatever is the latest fad, or craze, depending on how it is presented.

Whoredoms is when we chase after the latest anything--, the latest song, the latest artist, the latest and maybe the loudest political figure, the latest food or beverage. Anything and anyone can be made into an idol. And the fact that we or anyone else chases idols means that there is *whoredoms* in us and we need deliverance. Those with *whoredoms* raging in them are easily seduced by **strange fire** from strange altars that send strange humans, if they can be called that, into their lives. These strange altars may demand worship, and too often, getting it. Why do they get it? The people don't know, they are bewitched, and they are seduced; the *whoredoms* in them answers the *strange* call.

Verse 26

The altar of sex is huge. Sex altars can be found in so many places that it is almost unreal. In the world of marketing, those who sell and market anything at all— anything--, know that sex sells. Increasing *whoredoms* with the Egyptians through sexual indulgences is how *whoredoms* gets a foothold in people. Sex altars are often the "high places" built on every street corner. There could be soothsayers and diviners on street corners, there could be brothels and houses of ill-repute, and there could be drug houses and *speakeasy's* where people literally get high, on street corners. Witchcraft, false churches, street walkers, brothels, and houses of sorcery are all altars.

When the Word says there are high places, the Word is truthful. All of this exalts itself against the knowledge and will of God for our lives.

As a teen, I recall seeing TV ad after ad telling me how I should look, what to wear, what makeup to wear, how to wear my hair even. Now that I'm not a teen, I can look back and see what that has gotten me--, nothing. If anything, trouble, but mostly nothing. Those sales campaigns were telling me how to look sexy, sensual and worldly. And what would that attract? A fellow after temporal, sensual and worldly engagements. I didn't think my parents were negligent then, but I rather wish I hadn't been left alone with my device—the TV set to tell me all this stuff that wasn't expedient for my life, with no other sound, Christian voice to counter those marketing words.

That *device* got me essentially, nothing—, maybe situationships that I would then have to figure out how to get out of. And, until I learned about soul ties and spiritual entanglements it would create iniquity that I would suffer through and if not repented of, my children would then inherit iniquity from my years of stupidity, rebellion, disobedience and sin.

Parents, what is your child or teen watching online, on TV or on their cellphone? If you don't correct what they see and hear with the Word of God, the Word of Truth and some good old common sense, they may grow up believing what those ads promote. And, what will that get them? Either nothing, or a world of hurt and disappointment. Media ads do not encourage godliness, as a rule.

Instead, *spirits* seduce, they choose to induce sales of products, not so much to corrupt a child or a teen, but that is the devil's underlying strategy.

Spirits seduce people to look a certain way, dress a certain way. Hair, attire, and attitude--, making a person look like a *strange altar*. Tattoos, muscle building, surgeries, etc. Of course, *whoredoms* influences a person to do all these things seamlessly most of the time making the victim think that this is their idea. Through demonic anointing they come to live in the person's soul, marrying them and marrying them to the idea so strongly that they feel they must do whatever they are instructed, inducted or initiated to do.

It's a two-way street, what's in you dictates to you how to dress and what to look like. And, also what you choose to wear, invites the *spirits* that like that sort of outfit, those types of tattoos, that color of hair and that style of hair. Sometimes the weave in your head is the marker that says to a demon—she's one of ours. Men, you are not exempt, men get weave too and depending on where it came from, whether or not it was prayed over, and most often it is not, and who put their hands on you to put it in your head, you could have invited a whole family reunion of demons into your life and your soul. You won't know until you know.

Tamar changed her clothes; she took off the clothes of the widow that she may have been wearing for at least a year or more and changed into the clothes and attire of a harlot. She attracted Judah who must have frequented harlots anyway, but at least on this particular trip he was looking for a streetwalker for some throwaway sex. That's actually impossible, as people may learn either every day, or eventually because sin has repercussions. Sex has repercussions. Not getting pregnant and not having a baby does not mean you got away with the sex.

Back in those days what you wore said who you were. She wore the clothes of a harlot, so she became one, and Judah saw her along the way and treated her like a harlot. In the movie, *Trading Places*, when Eddie Murphy and Dan Akroyd's characters changed places, they also changed their style of clothes. Or, shall I say when they changed their style of dress it was indicative that they had changed positions socio-economically and possibly spiritually?

Demons can make you do things that you might now otherwise do, want to do, or even think of doing. It is called bewitchment or seduction.

I don't know about you, but I have noticed that when I exercise, I don't crave ridiculous food. When I don't exercise, I want everything that is bad for me. It can be called comfort food, but who is it comforting?

The demons inside you.

Exercise does not make you crave ice cream. Nope. After exercising, the body usually feels so good and energized. There is oxygen flowing in the body.

They say it is impossible for a cancer cell to live in the presence of oxygen. Can it also be   true that demons hate oxygen—we know they hate light. For humans, oxygen is necessary for life. Demons do not sponsor or foster life, so the opposite must be true; they bring death and live in dark places and dark hearts. Shall we not surmise then that they also hate oxygen and cannot influence you to eat ice cream and other foods that are not good for you when you are lit up with the Word of God and oxygenated by your moving and breathing and having *life--*, the life of God in you?

God looks on the inside, at the heart. Godly men do as God does, they are not turned by sparkles and shines and baubles, although they appreciate beauty. A balance must be struck not to look like a harlot or a street walker if you are trying to attract a Godly mate.

Verse 27

Whoredoms can cause the diminishing of the value of food. This may be because of poverty and may lead to hunger and malnutrition in the natural, or by not being able to digest and absorb the nutrients from the food that you actually eat. **This opens up a whole new line of thought and understanding. Can *whoredoms* be the root of or contribute to GI and digestive issues?** Millions upon millions suffer from GI upset, disorders, and diseases. Witchcraft attack can greatly affect a GI tract--, you'd better believe this. Deliverance ministers will tell you that when the GI tract is hit and may begin to die, it is the beginning of the individual

beginning to die. Don't fall despondent here—, instead, pray. Seek God; He can heal whatever has come upon you. Repent and pray for healing, in the Name of Jesus
.

> Whose end is destruction, whose God is their belly, and whose glory is in their shame, who mind earthly things.
> (Philippians 3:19)

Greed and *lust* travel together. Don't believe it? It's true; people who are always hungry and eat anything and almost anywhere are subject to get trapped like a mouse searching for cheese that is in a trap. Spiritual food. Not blessing the food you eat is defiling. *Whoredoms.* The devil said, *Turn these stones into bread. Whoredoms.* Were all three of the temptations an attempt to introduce *whoredoms* into Jesus Christ???

The devil tried to tempt Jesus into turning stones into bread in John 6:26, 31. Jesus had been driven into the wilderness; He had fasted 40 days and was hungry. Typical devil; he was after that belly. Jesus didn't fall for it and Jesus is our supermodel.

Verse 28

Other hallmarks of the *spirit of whoredoms* are being insatiable and unsatisfied. This dissatisfaction may be with food and may cause a person be become overweight. A person could be insatiable sexually and overcome by sexual lust, or a lust for money, or fame.

The spirit of dissatisfaction is a real frustration. W*horedoms* makes a person think that there is no more--, or there is never enough. This leads to desperation, and desperation leads to stupid and desperate decisions, which most of the time include sin.

We serve El Shaddai, the One God who is More Than Enough. If the *spirit of enough* is not in you, then you may be subject to this demon that makes you chronically dissatisfied.

Verse 29

This *seducing spirit* can increase dissatisfaction by multiplying *whoredoms* with the world. These verses speak of the Assyrians and Chaldeans (Babylon). Babylon is of course, the world. When we look at worldly things sometimes folks get jealous and they want what the worldly man has – his mansions, his cars, his sailboat, who am I kidding? His yacht, his vacations and his bank account. The very lustful want his wife, or his women.

This sounds like a list of answers from a game show.

Anyhow--,

When I was a teenager, I overcame feelings of jealousy this way, and maybe it will help you. Ask yourself, when you see something that someone else has, are you willing to exchange everything you are and everything you have to acquire that one thing? The answer should be, No. If you are willing to exchange all, don't say it out of your mouth. Don't think on that thing that you don't have that you think you want or can't live without too long, because the devil will come along and make that happen too. In the New Testament idolatry is described as covetousness. Can you now see how all of this is tied together?

So, to the question, would you be willing to give up all that you are in exchange to be like someone else, or to become as they are?

The answer should be No, you are not willing to lose, exchange, or change everything about yourself and your life for that one thing. If you do it smacks of desperation and not knowing who you are and what you have in God. Seek deliverance. Today.

Verse 30

It is the spirit of a man that will sustain him in any trouble. Weakness of heart and mind is a curse and symptom of *whoredoms*. The spirit of a man has not been built up, but the flesh has, that speaks of *whoredoms*. The flesh has been seduced and has been catered to, which has resulted in the flesh being grown and overgrown.

If or when affliction hits that man, he has no defense if his spirit man has not been increased, but instead his soul and/or flesh are overgrown.

His soul?

Yes. His emotions can't sustain him, Most likely they have to be put in check. He cannot *will* his way through the afflictions of life, such as a witchcraft attack, and he cannot think his way out of one. The witchcraft attack, for example has already studied what your intellectual response will be to the attack. That has already been factored in and what your brain tells you to do, if it is not totally hijacked by the attack itself, will make the fallout from the attack even worse than if you do nothing.

The only answer in a witchcraft attack, occultic or other spiritual attack is to do only what Jesus would do.

What is that?

Read your Bible and either find out now, or better, know already because you have studied to show yourself approved. Amen.

Verse 32

Seducing spirits lead to adultery, and fornication as well as other sexual sins, but that's no newsflash. The adulterer may have become cold and callous by now, surely it is not their first time. So afterward, they may just wipe their mouth and keep it moving.

Just your mouth? This is so nasty.

Verse 33

Being contrary, causing dissensions, being hard or impossible to get along with are also characteristics of *whoredoms*.

People like this like to keep some mess going, it gives them pleasure. It gives them a sense of control while they manipulate all the people and the emotions of all the people around them. Yes, it is a form of witchcraft whether they realize they are doing it or not. Behaving this way is built in with the *whoredoms* as a defensive tool so when the offender is asked about his or her doings, the contrary *spirits* rise up and deflect whoever is asking. All this confusion is built in with *whoredoms*. It may work against humans, but God is not confused by any of these *spirits*.

These seducing spirits are dangerous; they fight progress. They frustrate even the best of intentions. These spirits kill relationships. They sponsor division, and work against unity. In unity is where God commands the blessing, so if you are in the opposite of unity, that is in disunity, then you are not blessed; no blessings have been commanded over your life.

Verses 37-41

No one should ever want to be at the place where they lose God's protection. God hates idolatry; *whoredoms* is a strongman and it sponsors idolatry among other sins. God is gracious and kind and longsuffering, but when He has had enough, He has had enough. Please don't let that be you who has run out of Grace in God's eyes because of *whoredoms* and having no walls built up against *seducing spirits*. Please don't be a person using *seducing spirits* to influence others, even into doing nice things for you that you think are harmless things.

Such as?

Serving you a glass of water or iced tea is one *such as.*

Pastor is being nice at church to get you to sign up for the committee to do whatever that committee is supposed to do is another type of *such as*.

Faking nice is still a *seducing spirit* in operation. Once any *spirit* is invited in, it wants to stay, so this is real danger.

Weekly, at least and sometimes daily I see or hear someone come into my office, with a hearty *Good morning, how are you* – and a big smile. I know this is fake because people aren't kind and gracious and friendly like they once were. Immediately I know that this is a salesperson. That is a salesperson with a *seducing spirit*. No, I'm not saying that all salespeople have *seducing spirits*.

But, they can.

How will you make a sale if you aren't at least nice? It's just that when your nice is fake that is the lying, *seducing spirit* operating through you. If you are going to be friendly, nice, and pleasant BE that. Be for real, keep it real and this way there is no way the devil can send or fit a *seducing spirit* into your life to embed itself like a parasite, like a tick into your soul.

Verse 45

Whoredoms will drag a man or a woman away from their marriage, their family and their homes. Don't get it twisted, a witch can send a curse to effect that very outcome, but a curse, causeless cannot alight. There must be a sin or a sin nature in a man (or a woman) that will make that curse sent settle on that man and remove him from his relationship with his wife, his children and his life.

And being that it is a *seducing spirit*, he won't know what hit him or even why he is doing this destructive thing, dismantling his own life. He is just doing it. What is presented to him as an option instead of his wife and children, and even the life he has built for himself may be exactly what he has been fantasizing about. Or, saints of God, it may not be anything that he has ever been attracted to or interested in in his very life. He just knows he **must** do it, he has to do it, without spiritual walls up he will be compelled to do what is presented to him, especially if what is presented matches what is in his blood. If *whoredoms* is in him, when a *seducing spirit* such as *whoredoms* from the outside of him calls, he will answer it. To what degree it is sent and with what power and intent will determine if he strays, if he strays once, if he strays often, or if he completely strays and loses his way back home.

It also depends on what his wife will tolerate. Some wives give no strikes. Some wives call themselves forgiving, and allow one. Some two, and others just keep hoping that he will *change*.

Folks, if hope could change a man, Jesus wouldn't have had to come here and die to save us. The Spirit of the Lord would not have had to be released to set the captives FREE if hope could fix all of this.

Having *whoredoms* or any demon in your soul makes you captive. Period.

Loathing and rejecting husband and children is part of *whoredoms*; people are seduced into this ungodly behavior. Rejecting God, divorce, and broken families are other curses and result of the seducing idolatrous *spirit* and strongman of *whoredoms*.

Verse 47

Whoredoms will make a person appear more corrupt in God's sight than the heathen.

When I was in high school the teacher handed me back an essay one day and I had a B on it. My friends, whom I know couldn't put together an essay like I could also had B's and B+, one of them even had an A. Boldly, I stayed after class and asked the teacher why didn't I have an A on my paper?

She looked at me puzzled.

I doubled-down and said, *The other kids---, my friends aren't as good in this subject as I am.* (I was very confident that day.)

She cut me off and said, *You got a B because you can do better. Your friends got the grades they got based on how well they could write.*

Stunned, I turned around and left the classroom.

When God says that His people are more corrupt in His sight than the heathen, He is saying quite a bit. First of all, heathens are heathens, so they do what heathens do. Secondly, God expects **more** of us whom He has saved, sanctified, washed away the polluted blood that we have wallowed in. He has beautified and adorned us and put His Holy Spirit in us—all who have submitted to Him and all who have asked.

We should know better.

We should do better.

We should *be* better.

Judgment begins in the House of God for a reason. And that reason is that we should *be* better.

Verse 49

Again, I mention the movie, **Trading Places.** The well-off stockbroker was framed for a crime and had to switch places with an uneducated con artist. As the Dukes, Randy and Mortimer had in their manipulating the two lives of these unsuspecting men, wagered that each in their certain positions would take on the characteristics of a person in that particular status in life.

And they did.

Eddie Murphy, who was promoted by favor for no apparent reason, became bougie. Dan Akroyd, who was demoted because of being framed unfairly became desperate.

Pride, fullness of bread, overeating, gluttony, self-indulgence, abundance of idleness; not helping the poor and needy described Dan Ackroyd's character in the movie, when he was well off and on top. Eddie Murphy's character became this way when he finally got money. Some are so excited about what they have in life they talk about it all the time. They talk about their accomplishments, not realizing that the more they talk about these trappings, the more they identify that they are trapped, whether they hear themselves talking, or not.

I heard a preacher say she took herself to dinner and it cost 1500 euros. This price was for one person. I'm not sure of the reason, but that seems excessive to me. Wine and champagne can drive the price of a meal up substantially; was she also drinking? She didn't say, but she continued to tell on herself.

Why?

I don't know.

It's not like Judas complaining of the precious ointment in the alabaster box to be sold and given to the poor, because she surely didn't come to that church to give in the offering, but instead, to raise one (or more) for herself. This preacher lady had to know that she could have had a very nice meal for $100, maybe even $50. No, she spent enough to feed a family of four for a month or better and then had the nerve and the haughtiness to brag about it.

Whoredoms.

Most likely though, people who are not used to anything, not used to having money talk like that. In her case has she not made her belly her *god* and the extravagant meal was worship?

Worship?

She put **money** on it--, that's worship.

Verse 50

Haughtiness and the commission of abominations may also come with this evil spirit. The proud are prideful in what they have accomplished, but the haughty are more like the folks who are born privileged and feel that they are better and different than others. Oh, but we humans do get comfortable, don't we? And when we get comfortable, we tend to get fat in our comforts.

A comfortable person feels secure. They don't think anything will happen to him. He doesn't think that anything will change. He is trusting in himself, he is trusting in his wealth, he is trusting in his position, money, and/or power. In his mind, he has promoted himself to king--, at least some kind of king. We may think that we are the king of our own territory, our own kingdom and our own realm. We think we have power.

God has the power. Power belongs to God. When we scale the ladder of power, the power that belongs to God the only way down if we don't fall under conviction for being wrong, we may have to be knocked down.

Pride cometh before a fall and haughtiness before destruction. If there is a fall or destruction in the offing, or around the corner, what will fall or be destroyed is already cursed. Pride is a curse. It takes pride to act out *whoredoms* unless someone is forcing you into *whoredoms*. As spoken of earlier, people who want to sin want to be seduced into the sin so they can use the seduction as an excuse. They can't. That is foolish; the iniquity and other fallout for sinning will still be present no natter who started it. No matter who initiated it, no matter who insisted or forced it. Demons still get transferred and iniquity still accrues.

Stay away from evil folks and evil situations.

Verses 52, 54

More are the children of *whoredoms* than you may have imagined. The Bible tells us: shame, being confounded, disappointed, delayed, ashamed, and becoming spiritually dry all fall under the curse of those who carry the spirit of *whoredoms* or hae it lodged in their souls or in their foundation or bloodline.

When you exhibit any of the above symptoms or signs, suspect *whoredoms* so you will know what you need to be delivered from. If you are praying for others and you see these signs, pray against the *seducing spirit* of *whoredoms*.

Verse 59

Whoredoms will draw you away and cause you to despise even promises and oaths you've made to God and will lead a person to ultimately break covenant with Him.

In the end, if you choose to forget your other lovers, idols, sins, and selfish desires and put your full faith in God, He will welcome you back. However, that has to be done on this side of death; there is no repentance after death. There is no one in hell to show you Mercy.

If you call on Him too late be may have to forget you even if you call yourself by His name. In the last days seven women will ask one man to be called by his name but they will take care of themselves financially. These women are basically saying that they will be wives *on paper* (I paraphrase) only, not real wives. God is not interested in fake friends, fake converts, fake followers, and especially not fake *brides*. After all, God has a Son who is looking for a Bride.

Can't trick God—none of us can. And, all of us together cannot trick Him either.

Jezebel

We can't leave out Jezebel, she is a great seducer. The prophets who ate at her table were influenced to do her bidding and of course she only asked that evil things be done on her behalf or to achieve her evil goals. Ahab was her husband, and he was a king; therefore, Jezebel was up there in rank--, she was a queen.

An evil *spirit* is bad enough, but an evil *spirit* in a person of power and position can be devastating. An evil *spirit* or group of them sometimes is the reason a person is in power--, they've influenced the person to power. So, idolatry can be in leadership, or the leadership is a result of the idolatry.

Evil councils, unopposed can run the world. If a person worships idols and does so full throttle, the idols that is the evil councils can give a man position, power and his evil heart's desire. Of course, this is with a price—most often his life and the life of his children, but he can get it. The one who is willing to play ball, even with demons, is too many times the ones we see rise to power. Not just men, women can also rise to power this way--, like Jezebel.

But don't twist this either, Jezebel is a spirit, not a gender. The *spirit of Jezebel* can be in a male or a female. Just know that if there is a Jezebel somewhere, there is an Ahab who is passive and weak and letting Jezebel have *her* way.

Son of man, these leaders have set up idols in their hearts. They have embraced things that will make them fall into sin. Why should I listen to their requests?

Tell them, 'This is what the Sovereign LORD says: The people of Israel have set up idols in their hearts and fallen into sin, and then they go to a prophet asking for a message. (Ezekiel 14:1-2 NLT)

Idols in their hearts are speaking of what is in their souls. The idols that a man carries are in his soul, the enemy is within, saints of God. The enemy has to be put out of our souls. God will deliver us but we have to ask for it, agree to kick those idols out and submit to the deliverance process. Deliverance doesn't have to be dramatic and in front of a TV congregation. Deliverance can come automatically when Truth is heard and faith for that Truth comes. There are many ways a person can receive deliverance and it is not embarrassing or painful. Instead, it is liberating.

So I, the LORD, will give them the kind of answer their great idolatry deserves. 5I will do this to capture the minds and hearts of all my people who have turned from me to worship their detestable idols.
(Ezekiel 14:4B, NLT)

In His Grace and Mercy, the Lord gives us the way out of the bondages that we place and find ourselves in.

Therefore, tell the people of Israel, 'This is what the Sovereign LORD says: Repent and turn away from your idols, and stop all your detestable sins. (Ezekiel 14:6, NLT)

This verse confirms to us that we must do something to get *seducing spirits* such as *whoredoms* out of our hearts, not just pray and tell the Lord to do it. Yes pray, but there is some resistance and warfare that we must do, ourselves.

I, the LORD, will answer all those, both Israelites and foreigners, who reject me and set up idols in their hearts and so fall into sin, and who then come to a prophet asking for my advice. I will turn against such people and make a terrible example of them, eliminating them from among my people. Then you will know that I am the LORD.(Ezekiel 14:7-8 NLT)

The above verse makes it more than clear that God is not playing with anyone. If anyone is a prophet or proclaims to be a prophet, then the ownness is on that man or woman of God to be a true prophet and never make false proclamations. Especially never say that God said a thing that He did not say. Else, God will later deal with that prophet. Ascribing something evil to God that He did not say or do is blasphemy. Conversely giving other than God glory for something good that God did is also blasphemy.

> False prophets and those who seek their guidance will all be punished for their sins. In this way, the people of Israel will learn not to stray from me, polluting themselves with sin. They will be my people, and I will be their God. I, the Sovereign LORD, have spoken!'" (Ezekiel 14:10-11, NLT)

Man wants to know the future, so he wants a prophet – at least he thinks he does. So, he finds one, or more in some cases. There are prophets, there is prophetic grace, there is the office of prophet. Without the Holy Spirit and discernment, how will a man know a true prophet of God from a false one? How will a man know the difference between a prophet and a diviner?

Pray to receive the Holy Spirit, saints of God!

God calls prophets; they are one of the five-fold ministry gifts to the Body of Christ. Some people call themselves into ministry. If God hasn't introduced you and said, **This is my son in whom I am well pleased**, then who has made your introduction? This doesn't have to be on the lines of John the Baptist baptizing Jesus in the Jordan River, and the dove alighting on the Christ with God's voice speaking from Heaven, but God will empower someone somehow, someplace to let it be known that He approves and has sanctioned your ministry.

And you need to be serious about serving the Lord in Spirit and in Truth, else, as I heard a pastor say once, you just have a work permit to do kingdom business, but God never really hired you.

The woman with the *spirit of divination* in the Book of Acts comes to mind; she was announcing Paul and the other Apostles, and she was accurate, but that was second heaven knowledge and God doesn't "hire" people and give them second heaven knowledge and loose them to spread that muck all around. That person with the *divining spirit* is a true *seducing spirit.* A little truth will soon be well-sprinkled with a lot of lies and lead people into error. That little truth may lead people to follow her and then the lies will start, but she will have already earned some followers and become an Influencer who can then easily lead so many into error and destruction.

We all must ask ourselves where is our faith that we have to know the future before the future becomes the present? Why don't we trust God as He said to do? Why don't we trust God by faith? Seeking after signs, wonders, and prophets to make our life easy, or to give us a head start on others--, *why?*

Sadly, if we are not seeking a Word from the Lord to get ahead of the devil, then what are we doing? We are just competing with people--, other individuals, whom we are not supposed to be warring against, or I'll say competing against because isn't competition, war? Isn't a war, competition?

So, we want to hear good things from the prophet. The people proclaimed,

Prophesy to us lightly, tell us what we want to hear (Isaiah 30:10)

False words obtained via crystal balls, horoscopes, runes and other forms of fortune telling are divination and are not prophecy, most often it is fluffy happy stuff. It's so you will like the diviner and go back to see them. If anything dramatic arises, it is to scare you to going back to see the false prophet, diviner or fortuneteller. It is all manipulation. Every time you see such a person, you get assigned a *familiar spirit* that now follows **you,** whereas you may have been going to the diviner to find out what another person was doing and asked that **they** be spiritually followed.

This is demonically ironic.

The woman (girl) with the *spirit of divination* had made her masters so much money. People will more quickly pay for divination than they will put money on a Godly altar spouting truth. Cleo knows.

Lord, what is wrong with us?

Judgment

Then this message came to me from the
LORD: "Son of man, suppose the people of
a country were to sin against me, and I
lifted my fist to crush them, cutting off
their food supply and sending a famine to
destroy both people and animals
(Ezekiel 14:12-13)

Or suppose I were to send wild animals to
invade the country, kill the people, and
make the land too desolate and dangerous
to pass through. ...
(Ezekiel 14:15A)

Or suppose I were to bring war against
the land, and I sent enemy armies to
destroy both people and animals.
(Ezekiel 14:17)

Or suppose I were to pour out my fury by
sending an epidemic into the land, and
the disease killed people and animals alike
(Ezekiel 14:19)

Now this is what the Sovereign LORD
says: How terrible it will be when all four
of these dreadful punishments fall upon
Jerusalem—war, famine, wild animals,
and disease—destroying all her people
and animals. (Ezekiel 14;21)

All those who make idols are worthless,
and the *gods* they prize so highly are
useless. Those who worship these *gods* are
blind and ignorant — and they will be
disgraced. It's no good making a metal
image to worship as a god!
(Isaiah 44:9)

Know ye not that the unrighteous shall
not inherit the kingdom of God? Be not
deceived: neither fornicators, nor
idolaters, nor adulterers, nor effeminate,
nor abusers of themselves with mankind,
(1 Corinthians 6:9-11)

God's judgment upon you is worse
than being at the mouth of hell. As soon as
God's hand is off you the devil is couched
at the door. As soon as you sin you are

game, and it is open season. The devil hunts men – did you not know it? The devil is still going to and *fro* in the Earth to see whom he may devour. Is he not then, a **hunter**?

If the devil is after you, God can help you. God can save you. God can deliver you.

If God is after you, *baby,* you don't have a chance because no man can help you against the Lord. Know for sure that the devil is not stronger than God. If you're falling under judgment with God without the possibility to repent—you're finished. Unless there is still time and room to repent and turn back to the Lord, it's too late.

Break the Curses of
Whoredoms

1. Lord, have Mercy on me, a sinner. If I am none of Yours give me a godly sorrow for my sins and a repentant heart and make me one of Yours. I believe that Jesus is the Son of God and He came to Earth to carry our sin to the Cross and redeem us back to the Father. He was crucified and on the third day God raised Him from the dead, and He lives. I believe in my heart, and I confess with my mouth that this is true, and Jesus is Lord. Now I am saved, Amen.
2. Lord, fill me with the Holy Spirit, with the evidence of speaking in tongues, in the Name of Jesus.

3. Holy Spirit Fire Fall on these prayers, in the Name of Jesus.

4. Blood of Jesus, cover me as I enter into this warfare, in Jesus' Name.

5. Lord, have Mercy; I repent for the sins of my parents and my ancestors back to Adam & Eve, where I retrieve my glory and essence, in the Name of Jesus.

6. Lord, in the Name of Jesus, I command any wicked power appointed to obstruct my path to fall down and die by force.

7. Lord, heal my foundation. Break up any evil in my foundation and rebuild it to Your specs. Heal my foundation in Jesus' Name.

8. In the Name of Jesus scatter any evil guardian in my path by Thunder, in the Name of Jesus. Let all evil groups plotting against me begin to kill one another, in the Name of Jesus.

9. In the Name of Jesus, I put on the garment of Fire to pass through every evil barrier.

10. In the Name of Jesus, let my prayers carry Fire through every evil gate of the wicked.

11. In the Name of Jesus, open everlasting doors that have been closed against me by wicked *spirits.*

12. In the Name of Jesus, let the powers of Heaven arise and lead me to the Throne of Grace.

13. I break the curses of *whoredoms* and order the evil covenants keeping curses in place against me to be shredded. Let those roots be dug up and destroyed, in Jesus' Name.

14. I command the curses, *whoredoms* and iniquities to be lifted from me and all my descendants, in the Name of Jesus.

15. Every *seducing spirit* and *spirit of whoredoms* attack, back to senders, (X3) in the Name of Jesus.

16. Every *spirit* blocking me from doing good works--, the works of the Lord, be bound, in the Name of Jesus.

17. *Every seducing and whoredom spirit* at the gate of my deliverance preventing me from entering in, be lift up (X3).

Lift up your heads, O ye gates; and be ye lift up, ye everlasting doors; and the King of glory shall come in. Who is this King of

glory? The Lord strong and mighty, the
Lord mighty in battle.
(Psalm 24:7-8)

18. In the authority and in Christ, I bind this
seducing spirit, whoredoms, and cut him
off at the source of his power, in the
Name of Jesus.

19. In the Name of Jesus, I *loose perverse
spirits, spoiler spirits,* hornets, Fire,
Burning Destruction and the Terror of
the Lord upon that strongman. all his
helper *spirits*, all of his associated
demons, and all other devils, and imps
under his control, in the Name of Jesus.

Some preceding prayers are from or adapted from
Joseph C. Okafor's book, **Unmasking Idolatry**.

20. Lord, I suffer not a demon to speak. I
silence the voice of every *seducing
spirit* sent to me, in the Name of Jesus.

21. I challenge and silence the voice of every *lying spirit* sent into my environment, in the Name of Jesus.

22. Lord, I bind any *spirit* within me that will hear, heed, or respond to a *seducing spirit* in the Name of Jesus, and I command that *spirit* or those *spirits* to come out, come out, come up and out, in the Name of Jesus.

23. Whoredoms of any kind in me, die, in the Name of Jesus (X7).

24. I command any *seducing spirit* and associated *spirits* to leave me, go to the Abyss where there is no water and there is no return, in the Name of Jesus.

25. *Lying spirits,* get out, in the Name of Jesus.

26. *Spirit of lust,* get out, in the Name of Jesus.

27. *Spirit of greed,* get out, in the Name of Jesus.

28. *Spirit of the lust for money* get out, in the Name of Jesus.

29. *Spirit of vain pride*, I bind you and cast you out of my soul and my life, in the Name of Jesus.

30. *Spirit of selfish pride*, I bind you and cast you out of my soul and my life, in the Name of Jesus.

31. *Spirit of hateful pride,* I bind you and cast you out of my soul and life, in the Name of Jesus.

32. *Spirit of the lust for fame* get out, in the Name of Jesus.

33. *Spirit of the lust for power*, get out, in the Name of Jesus.

34. *Anti-marriage spirit,* die, in the Name of Jesus.

35. Any *seducing spirit* sent to pull me away from my marriage or any other God-ordained relationship, die, in the Name of Jesus.

36. Any *seducing spirit* sent to pull me away from my child or children, walk away and die, in the Name of Jesus.

37. Any *seducing spirit* sent to bilk me out of money or property, die, in the Name of Jesus.

38. Any *seducing spirit* sent to get me to spend money where I shouldn't and on things not sanctioned by the Lord, die, in the Name of Jesus.

39. Any *seducing spirit* sent to block me from tithing, giving in offerings or sacrificing on Godly altars in a timely fashion, die, in the Name of Jesus.

40. Any *seducing spirit* sent to steal, block or delay blessings and favor the Lord has for me, die, in the Name of Jesus.

41. Any *seducing spirit* sent to make me to cause division or dissension in relationships or memberships that I am a part of, die, in the Name of Jesus.

42. Any *seducing spirit* sent to cause me to stray from sound Doctrine, die, in the Name of Jesus.

43. Any *seducing spirit* sent to cause me to leave where I should stay or stay where I should leave, die, in the Name of Jesus.

44. Any *seducing spirit* sent to seduce me into sexual sin of any kind, die, and leave my life, in Jesus' Name.

45. Every *seducing spirit* sent to initiate me into the kingdom of darkness, I silence you and I break any evil initiation, in the Name of Jesus.

46. Every *seducing spirit* sent with a message or evil instruction, I silence you and I cancel your evil instruction,

whether I **heard** it or not. I will NOT obey you or your instructions in the Name of Jesus.

47. Every *familiar spirit,* I bind you and command you to leave me, forever, in the Name of Jesus.

48. Every *monitoring spirit* sent to spy on me, I bind you from operating against me and I command you to give a lying report to your sender, in the Name of Jesus.

49. Every *seducing spirit* sent to seduce me to anything ungodly, die, in the Name of Jesus.

50. Any seducing spirit sent to block my ears, hearing or understanding, be cut off from your source of power and die, in the Name of Jesus.

51. Every *seducing spirit of distraction,* leave my life and die, in the Name of Jesus.

52. Any *seducing spirit* sent to divert my eyes and attention from what I should be

seeing to what I should not be looking at, die, in the Name of Jesus.

53. Thirst traps, fail against me, in the Name of Jesus.

54. Lord, deliver me from thirst traps, in the Name of Jesus.

55. Lord, deliver me from idolatry, deliver me from *whoredoms*, deliver me from cheating on You and everyone else in my life, in the Name of Jesus.

56. Itching ears and gossip be cast down in my life; Lord, let Your Truth reign supreme over me, in the Name of Jesus.

57. Anointed false words and lies, fall to the ground as dead works against me, in the Name of Jesus.

58. Every *seducing spirit* sent to draw me into sin, die, in the Name of Jesus.

59. Every *seducing spirit* sent to draw me to sickness, affliction, emotional or mental disorders, die, in the Name of Jesus.

60. Every *seducing spirit* sent to draw me to poverty, or to make unwise financial decisions, die, in the Name of Jesus.

61. Every *seducing spirit* sent to call me to death, the grave or hell, you go there, because I won't. I will live and not die, in the Name of Jesus.

62. Lord, deliver me from every Jezebellish outfit whether for home, work, and especially for church, in the Name of Jesus.

63. Lord, deliver me from Jezebel telling me what to wear, in the Name of Jesus.

64. Lord, deliver me from worldliness; deliver me from the world, in the Name of Jesus.

The following prayers against Jezebel are from Dr. John Eckhardt's **Prayers that Rout Demons**:

65. I *loose* the bounds of Heaven against the seducer, Jezebel, in the Name of Jesus. (1 Kings 21:23)

66. I rebuke and bind the *spirits of witchcraft, lust, seduction, intimidation, idolatry*, and *whoredoms* connected to Jezebel, in the Name of Jesus.

67. I release the *spirit of Jehu* against Jezebel and her cohorts, in the Name of Jesus (2 Kings 9:30-33).

68. I command Jezebel to be thrown down and eaten by the Hounds of Heaven, in the Name of Jesus.

69. I rebuke all *spirits of false teaching, false prophecy, idolatry*, and *perversion* connected with Jezebel, in the Name of Jesus. (Revelation 2:20)

70. I loose tribulation against the kingdom of Jezebel, in the Name of Jesus. (Rev 2:22)

71. I cut off and break the powers of every word released by Jezebel against my life, in the Name of Jesus.

72. I cut off Jezebel's table and reject all food from it, in the Name of Jesus. (1 Kings 18:19)

73. Father, I cut off and loose myself from all curses of Jezebel and *spirits* of Jezebel operating in my bloodline, in Jesus' Name.

74. I cut off the assignment of Jezebel and her daughters to corrupt my life, in Jesus' Name.

75. I rebuke and cut off the *spirit of Athaliah* that attempts to destroy the royal seed, in the Name of Jesus (1 Kings 11:1)

76. I rebuke and cut off the *spirit of whoredoms* in the Name of Jesus. (Hosea 4:12).

77. I rebuke and cut off Jezebel and her witchcrafts, in the Name of Jesus

78. .

79. I rebuke and cut off the harlot and mistress of witchcrafts and break her power over my life and family, in the Name of Jesus (Nahum 3:4)

80. I cut off witchcraft out of your hand and you will no longer cast spells, in the Name of Jesus. (Micah 5:12).

81. I overcome Jezebel and receive power over the nations, (Revelation 2:26)

Turn us again, O God, and cause thy face to shine; and we shall be saved.
(Psalms 80:3)

82. Lord, we renounce and denounce idolatry, whether to things, people, inanimate objects, stars--, anything, Lord, forgive us, in the Name of Jesus.

83. In the Name of Jesus, give my destiny express open heavens eternally.

84. My heavens which have been closed by the forces of Heaven, open today, in the Name of Jesus.

85. I declare and decree: Whatever parental sin has blocked my heavens, I am born again, I am in Christ, those blockages must die, in the Name of Jesus.

86. Lord, open my heavens now by Fire, in the Name of Jesus.

87. In the Name of Jesus Father, I command my life to begin operating under an open heaven.

88. In the Name of Jesus let every vile sacrifice against my open wide heavens perish, in the Name of Jesus.

89. Let Thunder silence all the evil words against my open heavens, in the Name of Jesus.

90. In the Name of Jesus, arise, O God's hand and open my locked heaven and let it remain opened forevermore, in the Name of Jesus.

91. Every witchcraft power that has tried to lock up my Heavens, you have failed. I command you to catch Fire and burn to ashes, in the Name of Jesus.

92. I command any authority in the celestial realms that is cursed to shut my heavens, somersault and die, in the Name of Jesus.

93. Lift up the heads of these gates and keep them open; they shall remain open, eternally for me and my bloodline, in the Name of Jesus.

94. Arrow of the Lord, pursue all my enemies full force, by Fire and by Force, in the Name of Jesus.

Lord, I seal these declarations and prayers across every dimension, realm, age, timeline, past, present, and future to infinity, in the Name of Jesus. I seal them with the Blood of Jesus and the Holy Spirit of Promise, Amen.

Any backlash because of these prayers, backfire to infinity, in the Name of Jesus.
I count it as done, Thank You, Lord.

AMEN.

Dear Reader

Thank you for acquiring and reading this book.

May the Lord deliver you swiftly from idolatry in any form, whether you realize it or not. This is especially important since God hates idolatry the most.

May He deliver you from any and every seducing spirit, and especially Jezebel and every curse of the *spirit of whoredoms,*

In the Name of Jesus,

Amen.

Dr. Marlene Miles

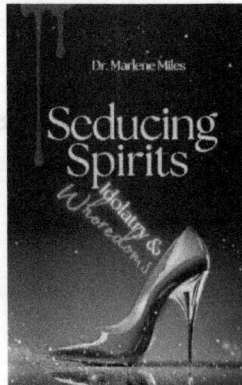

Prayer books by this author

While most books by this author have prayer points either throughout the book or at the end, there are some books that are **only** prayers. You just open up the book and pray. They are listed below:

Prayers Against Barrenness: *For Success in Business and Life*

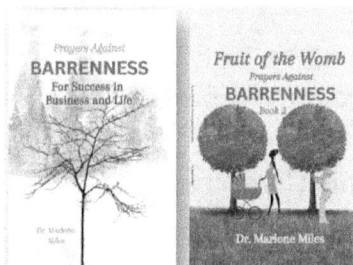

Fruit of the Womb: *Prayers Against Barrenness*

Beauty Curses, *Warfare Prayers Against*
https://a.co/d/5Xlc2OM

Courts of Marriage: Prayers for Marriage in the Courts of Heaven *(prayerbook)* https://a.co/d/cNAdgAq

Courtroom Warfare @ Midnight
(prayerbook) https://a.co/d/5fc7Qdp

Demonic Cobwebs *(prayerbook)*
https://a.co/d/fp9Oa2H

Every Evil Bird https://a.co/d/hF1kh1O

Gates of Thanksgiving

Soulish & Diabolical Prayer Treatment

Spirits of Death & the Grave, Pass Over Me and My House
https://a.co/d/dS4ewyr

*Please note that my name is spelled incorrectly on amazon, but not on the book.

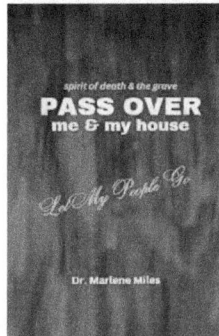

Throne of Grace: Courtroom Prayer

https://a.co/d/fNMxcM9

Warfare Prayer Against Poverty
https://a.co/d/bZ61lYu

Other books by this author

AK: *The Adventures of the Agape Kid*

AMONG SOME THIEVES

Ancestral Powers https://a.co/d/9prTyFf

Backstabbers https://a.co/d/gi8iBxf

Barrenness, *Prayers Against*
https://a.co/d/feUltIs

Battlefield of Marriage, *The*

Blindsided: *Has the Old Man Bewitched You?* https://a.co/d/5O2fLLR

Break Free from Collective Captivity

By Means of a Whorish Father

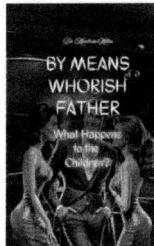

Casting Down Imaginations
https://a.co/d/1UxlLqa

Church Craft: Witchcraft In the Church

Churchzilla, The Wanna-Be, Supposed-to-be Bride of Christ

Curses of Blind Men

Demonic Cobwebs (prayerbook)

Demonic Time Bombs

Demons Hate Questions

Devil Loves Trauma, *The*

Devil Weapons: Unforgiveness, Bitterness,...

The Devourers: Thieves of Darkness 2

Do Not Swear by the Moon

Don't Refuse Me, Lord (4 book series)

https://a.co/d/idP34LG

Dream Defilement

The Emptiers: *Thieves of Darkness, 1*
https://a.co/d/5I4n5mc

Evil Touch https://a.co/d/gSGGpS1

Failed Assignment
https://a.co/d/3CXtjZY

Fantasy Spirit Spouse
https://a.co/d/hW7oYbX

FAT Demons (The): *Breaking Demonic Curses*

The Fold (5-book series)

- The Fold (Book 1)
- Name Your Seed (Book 2)
- The Poor Attitudes of Money (3)

- Do Not Orphan Your Seed (4)
- For the Sake of the Gospel (5)
- My Sowing Journal

Gang Ups: Touch Not God's Anointed

got HEALING? Verses for Life

got LOVE? Verses for Life

got HOPE? Verses for Life

got money? https://a.co/d/g2av41N

Hidden Sins: Hidden Iniquity

How to Dental Assist

How to Dental Assist2: Be Productive, Not Wasteful

Idols Are Demons, Idols Are Devils, Idols Are Little-g *gods*

I Take It Back

In Multiplying I Will Multiply Thee

Legacy

Let Me Have A Dollar's Worth
https://a.co/d/h8F8XgE

Level the Playing Field

Living for the NOW of God

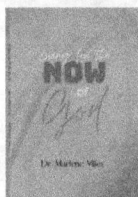

Lose My Location
https://a.co/d/crD6mV9

Man Safari, *The*

Marriage Ed. Rules of Engagement &
Marriage

Made Perfect in Love

Money Hunters: Beware of Those

Money on the Altar https://a.co/d/4EqJ2Nr

Mulberry Tree https://a.co/d/9nR9rRb

Motherboard (The)- *Soul Prosperity Series*

Name Your Seed

Occupy: *Until I Return*

Plantation Souls

Players Gonna Play

Power Money: Nine Times the Tithe

https://a.co/d/gRt41gy

The Power of Wealth *(forthcoming)*

Powers Above

Repent of Visiting Evil Altars

The Robe, Part 1, The Lessons of Joseph

The Robe, Part II, The Lessons of Joseph

Seasons of Grief

Seasons of Waiting

Seasons of War

Second Marriage, Third--, *Any Marriage*

https://a.co/d/6m6GN4N

Seducing Spirits: *Whoredoms*

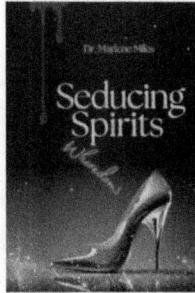

Sift You Like Wheat

Six Men Short: What Has Happened to all the Men?

SON

Soulish & Diabolical Prayer Treatments

Soul Prosperity soul prosperity series 3

https://a.co/d/5p8YvCN

Souls Captivity soul prosperity series 2

The Spirit of Poverty

StarStruck

SUNBLOCK

The Swallowers: *Thieves of Darkness*, 3

Take It Back

This Is NOT That: How to Keep Demons from Coming at You

Time Is of the Essence

Too Many Wives: *Why You Have Lady Problems*

Tormenting Spirits   https://a.co/d/dAogEJf

Toxic Souls

Triangular Power *(series)*

- Powers Above
- SUNBLOCK
- Do Not Swear by the Moon
- STARSTRUCK

Uncontested Doom

Unguarded Hours, *The*

Unseen Life, *The*
https://a.co/d/0drZ5Ll

Upgrade: How to Get Out of Survival Mode

- Toxic Souls (Book 2 of series)
- Legacy (Book 3 of series)

The Wasters: *Thieves of Darkness*, Bk 2
https://a.co/d/bUvI9Jo

What Have You to Declare? What Do You Have With You from Where You've Been?

When I Was A Child, *I Prayed As a Child*

When the Devourer is Rebuked

https://a.co/d/1HVv8oq

The Wilderness Romance *(series)* This series is about conducting a Godly relationship and marriage with someone who is a Wilderness person. It is about how to recognize it and navigate through it. These books are about how not to get caught up in such.

- *The Social Wilderness*
- *The Sexual Wilderness*
- *The Spiritual Wilderness*

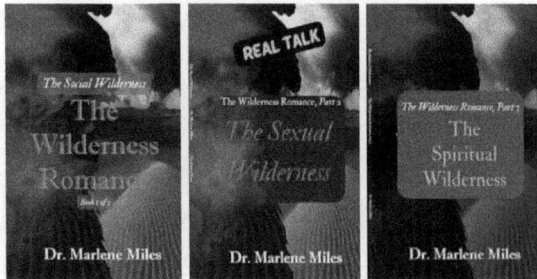

Other Series

The Fold (a series on Godly finances)
https://a.co/d/4hz3unj

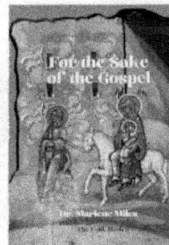

Soul Prosperity Series https://a.co/d/bz2M42q

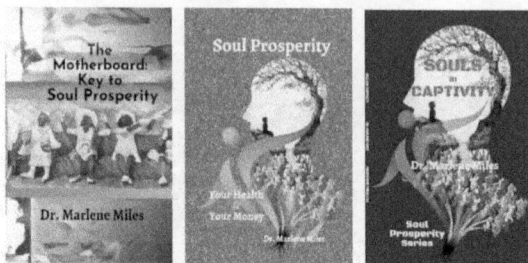

Spirit Spouse books

https://a.co/d/9VehDSo

https://a.co/d/97sKOwm

Thieves of Darkness series

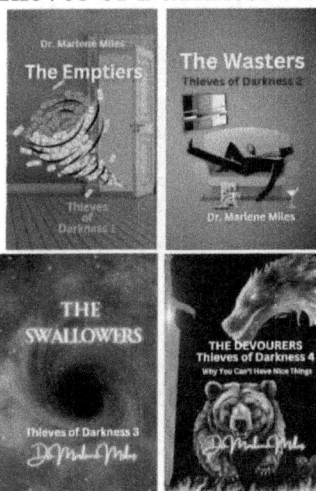

Triangular Powers https://a.co/d/aUCjAWC

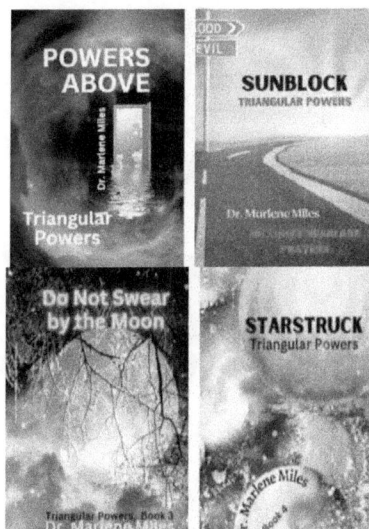

Upgrade (series) *How to Get Out of Survival Mode* https://a.co/d/aTERhXO

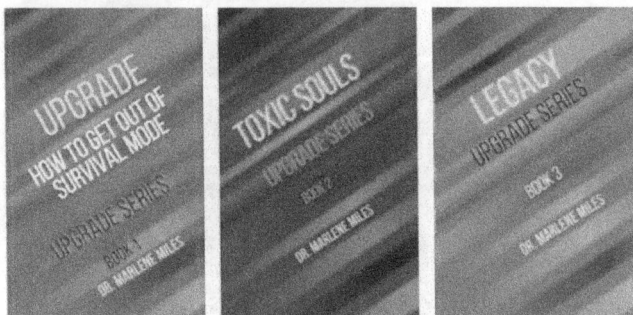

www.ingramcontent.com/pod-product-compliance
Lightning Source LLC
LaVergne TN
LVHW051241080426
835513LV00016B/1706